I0425794

M. J. Joachim's Book Review Guide

How to Get Positive Reviews for Your Book

About the Author

M. J.'s Writing Tips, Reviews and More blog contains in-depth reviews, free book promotions, lots of writing and a host of other things writing and author related. It's a place to read excellent reviews, learn about new books (even if M. J. hasn't had time to read and review them yet), and enjoy the creative, artistic aspects of writing. If you're interested in submitting a book review request or want to ask for your free book promotion, please read the following articles:

M. J.'s Open Letter to Authors Regarding Book Reviews

M. J.'s Free Publicity: Send Me Your Book Promos and Author Bios

Both of these posts will help you understand that M. J. is extremely passionate about what she does on her blog, and as a writer herself, loves helping other authors share their work and promote it. Naturally, she doesn't have the opportunity to help everyone, but she certainly reads a lot, posting as many book reviews and promotions as possible.

M. J. reads all genres in the interest of learning and expanding her literary horizons. Please feel free to contact her for consideration of your free book promotion and/or book review request. She is happy to be of service to authors, reading and promoting their books, and looks forward to getting to know authors and their works in turn. M. J. can be reached via email at:

mjjoachimswriting@gmail.com

Table of Contents

Introduction

It's that dream you've always had, or maybe it's that urge you can't seem to get away from, the thing that makes you tick, forcing you to make time for it, because writing is part of you, and you simply can't not do it. You have to write, because if you don't you won't be true to yourself, and you may well run the risk of suffocating some deep inner part of you, the part that promises life is not ordinary, recognizing the artistry in everyday living, seeing the beauty in the smallest of details and caressing the hope in the most dire situation.

You are a writer! As long as you write, you are content with the world around you. The moment you stop, you're lost feeling like there must be something more. So you wake up early, stay up late, skip the chores, call in sick to work, give up socializing, all because even the smallest amount of time, is enough to satisfy the urge, allowing you to poor words out on the page, imagining even the greatest of enemies can be your friend, and the worst of friends can still be forgiven in your story of hope and redemption. Or maybe that's not right. Maybe the greatest of enemies is the biggest villain that ever lived, and that worst of friends became that same biggest villain, someone you opt to murder for being such blight against humanity. It could go either way, you know, since you're the one putting the words upon the page.

Just when things start to get interesting in your story, you realize there's a whole lot of work to be done if this phenomenal story of yours is ever going to see the light of day. You suddenly feel overwhelmed with the seemingly endless list of things you should and shouldn't do, because it isn't enough to write your story. You instantaneously have a deep and burning desire to have someone, or maybe a few somebodies, read your book and tell you what they think about it. It's a daunting task asking someone to engage with you on the characters you've so carefully drafted, getting to know most of them better than your own family. After all, you've been emotionally and perhaps physically unavailable for months. You've been buried deep in the trenches, fixing every conceivable flaw on every leaf of every background, every blemish on every face. You even left a few imperfections on purpose, to add contrast and magnify depth in your story.

It wasn't easy coming to grips with these people and places you created. The entire process took hours, days, weeks or maybe even years. Intimacy is the understatement. You've not only seen these characters in their underwear, you've slowly and carefully undressed them completely, masterfully molding them into the perfect being in the most powerful place. Human, alien, animal, none of it matters, because your characters have come alive within your pages, forcing you to travel beyond your comfort zone, causing you to make your book public by publishing it, challenging you to submit your book for authoritative reviews, in the hopes of getting positive feedback, and maybe even starting a grassroots movement, where you catch the brass ring and reach the top of the charts in your genre.

Part 1: The Basics

Chapter 1: Consistency and Clarity

Fiction Books

Just because you know your characters and places inside and out, doesn't mean everyone else does. In all likelihood, your reader has never met or seen most, if not all of the things in your book – unless it's a series and your reader has been faithfully following along with each new installment. It's up to you to make the formal introductions, allowing anyone who picks up your book to feel like they know and see all, without wondering if they missed something, because you somehow forgot to fill them in on the finer details of what was going on in your imagination when you wrote your story.

Characters should be consistent within the parameters you've set forth for them, making them identifiable and relatable to your audience. This doesn't mean you shouldn't add that gut-wrenching twist, where your audience thinks the character is one way, only to find out he's completely the opposite of what they expected. If written well, this will heighten the drama and add volume to the story. Boring characters particularly benefit from consistency, because your audience knows they're boring, something that can be a really good thing, especially when they are paired in some dynamic duo, where opposites attract and their role is primarily supportive.

Consistency and clarity are important beyond character development, in that your dialog must make sense, and your backdrop should be logical and appropriate, fitting easily within the realms of the rest of your story. Introducing new elements that don't quite fit reads more like a tangent or an unnerving rant, than a consistent part of your story. If you decide to divert from the main story line for whatever reason, fill your audience in and be clear about what and why you are taking a detour. Easier said than done, because the words still must flow and be consistent with the rest of the story. Still, it can be done, and when it's done well, it can earn big bonus points on your reviews.

Non-Fiction Books

Non-fiction writers should also be consistent and clear in their manuscripts, opting to cite resources that are easily and readily found in their work. Non-fiction writers should never take their audience for granted, thinking that just because the author knows something, everyone else does too, or worse yet, everyone should take the author at his word. It simply doesn't work like that, in part because anyone can write and produce a book these days, but also because opinions are not facts, and non-fiction books need to be based on verifiable fact, without supposing that just because the author wrote and published it, the truth has been revealed. As if the truth were somehow shrouded in mystery before this particular author decided to enlighten everyone with his presupposed, self inflated knowledge.

Non-fiction books will in all probability, be exceedingly scrutinized by reviewers, because they are stating things as fact, indicating the room for error in the margin is decidedly small. Facts being what they are can readily be checked; any good reviewer will take the time to do so, particularly when things don't seem to add up, or are mere projections of an author's fantasy and grandiose idea of how things should be, as opposed to how they actually are in reality.

I'd like to share a bit of a funny story with you about reviewing non-fiction books now. You see the very first book I created via Create Space to publish on Amazon, came about as a result of reviewing a poorly written and factually mixed up non-fiction book. I never had any intention of writing a book on canning, let alone spending so many hours in my kitchen that extremely hot Arizona summer, but I grew up around canning, and I knew the information I was reading would mislead people and send them in the wrong direction.

Consequently, I took it upon myself to produce a reliable canning book that would clearly provide all the necessary details on hot water bath canning. It wasn't enough to search through my memories and explain the process, because my facts had to be exact, my materials had to be accurate and my process had to make sense, allowing anyone who wants to attempt home canning, to do so easily and with a clear and factual picture of how it's supposed to be done.

I spent hours in the kitchen experimenting with the process and taking notes to get it just right. My family was overwhelmed with how much produce I purchased in bulk, and how many mason jars graced our countertops and filled our pantry. No one complained, because the food was good. I canned everything from stew to chili, vegetables and fruits to pie filling, and we all tested my efforts proving that I not only nailed the process to a T, but also explained it accurately and effectively. This is what reviewers look for and expect when reading non-fiction books. However the research gets done, writers need to do whatever it takes to publish non-fiction books with the utmost accuracy and clarity.

Now, I'm not in the business of reading poorly written books and writing new ones myself, but this one hit a nerve, because if people accept poor cooking practices as the right way to do things, they could end up wasting a whole lot of food, or worse yet, get very sick from eating what they prepare. This particular poorly written canning book became an author's inspiration, and even if I didn't read it to post a review on my blog, I probably would have written my canning book after reading it anyway, because it stirred something in the writer in me, to take the time to do so.

Considering that the market is so saturated with books these days, it makes sense to do your research thoroughly. Non-fiction books need to have all the i's dotted, all the t's crossed and all the facts checked. It's an added step, but it will undoubtedly make the difference between a poor, so-so or excellent review.

Children's Books

Among the most consistent and clear things authors of children's books must consider, is setting a good example for the kids who are going to read them.

This means eliminating vague and inappropriate language, while providing sound and superior messages. Humor doesn't need to be base, and language should rightly set the bar high, teaching kids to interact respectfully among themselves and with others.

Proofreading and editing should be done to perfection when publishing children's books, because exposure to incorrect spelling and grammar could pose a problem for any student trying to master the basics. Usage of proper vocabulary is vital for kid's books, because as much as they need to expand their vocabulary, writers need to publish works consistent with their age level. It's okay to push them to learn more in one's book. It is not okay to talk way over their head or dumb down books in such a way that the reader feels inferior.

Picture books need to have engaging and colorful pictures. It doesn't matter if the illustrator uses a brown or charcoal palette to make the pictures. These are still colors, and they work well in the proper setting. Pictures, however, need to be formatted to fill the page, with the wording flowing as it should, from one page to the next, matching the story and keeping the interest of young children and those who read to them.

This is not to imply that authors and illustrators of picture books must follow specific, tightly bound rules when inserting pictures in their books. As with any good book, pictures can enhance the product, so if an author decides their pictures don't need to fill the page, that's okay, provided they accent the work effectively. Tiny pictures on a blank page that has a few words won't cut it. Picture books are called picture books for a reason.

Chapter 2: Formatting

And oh, how I hope there will be no glitches when I format and upload this book of mine! There is nothing more difficult to read than a poorly formatted book, where the font is all caddywampus, the words don't fit on the page correctly, the Table of Contents isn't in the front of the book, or worse yet doesn't exist at all.

With so many guides and instruction lists on how to properly format a book these days, there's no excuse for it either. Perhaps you'll need to do your homework and climb onto one of the biggest learning curves of your life, but that shouldn't stop you from formatting your book correctly.

Formatting is all-inclusive, including everything from the cover to the last page. Your book needs to look, act and be able to be treated like a book. Hard copy, paperback or ebook, your book needs to function exactly like a real book, the same type of book that has a cover, publisher page and copyright, title page, Table of Contents, the actual body of your book, indexes if required, lists of references if necessary, and all the other bells and whistles any book that has ever been published showcases to make things sequential, logical and easy to understand and reference by the reader.

Once all the parts and pieces are laid out appropriately, phase two of the formatting process can begin. Typeset needs to be standard, paragraphs can be indented, though it's not necessary in my opinion. Personally, I prefer a bit of white space, particularly in electronic books, so skipping a line between paragraphs, instead of indenting is a viable option, though from my understanding, most reviewers won't fault an author for submitting either format. That said, large sections of white space are not nearly as attractive or acceptable in ebook formats.

While ending a chapter on one page, and starting a new chapter on the next is common practice in print books, ebooks tend to get too many blank pages that way, so it can be a bit of a detriment, depending on how the individual reviewer feels about such things. Many reviewers will give the author the benefit of the doubt, and not be too picky about such things, but average readers might not be so lenient, and one must consider everyone in their audience. Average readers, along with tried and true reviewers, will be submitting and publishing reviews on your book, so as much as it might be a hassle, it's probably worth your while to minimize blank pages, particularly in ebook formats.

Chapter 3: Proofreading and Editing

Ah, the dreaded typo – please don't tout that you've had your book praised and proofed by beta readers, unless those same beta readers can actually catch a typo or grammatical error. Sloppy work deserves poor reviews, no matter how many people helped "polish" your concluding draft before final publication.

The best advice I can give is to slow down, step away and take your time producing your manuscript. It's not a race, and it won't be a good review if you cross the finish line with what appears to be more of a rough draft of your manuscript, than an actual professionally finished book you took time and sweat to publish. A little bit of pride in your work will go a long way when it comes to getting positive reviews. A lot of pride can be your downfall, especially when your actual work doesn't live up to all your hype about it.

Along with catching the obvious errors relating to spelling and grammar in your book, proofing and editing should be taken a step further. They should analyze the characters, making sure they stay true to form, conduct the fact checking, adjust the pictures, check to make sure any links work, and determine if the story is consistent and clear. Any necessary changes need to be made during the editing and proofreading process, which should not take place until the final rough draft is complete. Yes, I do believe in producing more than one rough draft, because you'd be amazed how many errors you can find, after sitting and staring at your first and second rough draft for days on end.

Once you've created a perfected manuscript, it's time to upload it to your publishing platform. Once again you are tasked with the tedious mission of formatting, editing and proofreading, except this time you're doing it using tools provided by the automated publishing service. If you are working with a traditional publisher, you will still need to do this step, though there may be middlemen to help turn your manuscript into an actual book.

Regardless of how many people are involved in the process, your name is the one going on the cover, so you need to spend as much time as necessary to get this final formatting, editing and proofreading perfected.

Part 2: Interacting with Reviewers

Chapter 4: Reviewer Critiques

It helps to remember that reviewers are actual writers just like you. The only difference is, they read your books and write reviews about what you wrote. Many of us actually write and publish books just like you do, so we know how tedious and time consuming the existing process of publishing a book can be. We also recognize sloppy work when we see it; any reviewer worth their salt is going to give a thumb's down to poorly written and constructed manuscripts.

As a reviewer, I don't shy away from writing negative reviews because I want the best books to advance in the ranks, make it to the top of the charts, thereby selling more books for their authors. I'm invested in seeing good books receive their accolades, while poorly written and produced books get upgraded by their authors, based on necessary suggestions made by anyone who sees a need for improvement in the manuscript. Short of fixing the obvious errors, poorly produced books should fall in the ranks, while the best books surge to the top of the charts.

Reviewer critiques are based on a number of things, not the least of which is an intriguing and engaging story. Authors must be prepared to submit the whole package – boxes, wrapping paper, bows and all. Everything must be bundled up in an exciting and tempting package meant to tantalize and engage readers, and produced with a professionalism that cannot be denied.

Reviewer critiques are written from a bird's eye view, because reviewers must be able to stand behind their work, so it is up to them to notice what the average reader might miss or ignore. It is up to the reviewer to hold the writer accountable for the production of his work. If you are submitting your manuscript to a reviewer, it is a very good idea to remember that reviewers will not take your submission lightly, and if they read and review your work, they will scrutinize it closely.

Getting a 5 Star review from a reviewer is not and shouldn't be an easy task, because as much as any good reviewer will try to remain objective, he will also read your work with the utmost care and attention, often considering what needs to be written in the review as he reads. I'm consistently making mental and sometimes physical notes, when reading a book I'm reviewing. I strive to make my reviews honest, accurate and fair, minimizing any personal opinions I might have about the work. If for some reason I need to include my personal opinion in a review, I try to do so with a disclaimer, stating that it is my opinion and not necessarily based on fact, encouraging readers of my reviews to form their own opinions, while taking mine in the spirit it was intended.

Negative reviews happen, sometimes regardless of whether or not they are merited. Some people like to play power trips, while others are having a bad day. It is in every reviewer's best interest to only give negative reviews to those books that truly are substandard, and need to be reworked in an edited and finely polished future edition. Unfortunately, this doesn't always happen, especially when the general public is reviewing books; it is in the author's best interest to seek out professional reviews of their manuscript for this very reason, because professional reviewers have an obligation to the author to try to remain as objective as possible.

Most professional reviews offer a mix of pros and cons about the book being reviewed, because it is their job to provide the larger audience with as much information as possible about the books they review. For this reason, when you are seeking reviews for your book, you should make a point to read several reviews by the same reviewer, while closely studying a valid sample that includes positive, negative and neutral reviews.

Chapter 5: Finding the Perfect Reviewer

There are as many ways to find the perfect reviewer for your book, as there are reviewers available to review it. One of the easiest ways is to do an Internet search using the words, "book reviewers." Once you do that, a list of sites, articles and resources appears, so then it's a matter of doing a bit of research and networking, to see which reviewer might be the best fit for you and your book. Keep in mind that if you've written multiple books across varying genres, you might need a different reviewer for each book you've written.

Other ways to find the perfect reviewer for your book are to check sites where reviews are posted regularly. Amazon has a top reviewer's list, and there are numerous reviews on Goodreads too. The task is tedious, but it's up to you to read as many of those reviews as possible, and determine which reviewer might be a match for you and your book.

It's important to scope out the territory, and get to know the reviewers through their reviews and other writings. An easy way to do this is to follow their blog and social media publications. You can tell a lot about a person, by the way they write and interact with others, so if you get a bad vibe for any reason, it might be a good idea to skip that one and move onto the next. Or maybe they simply don't seem as professional as you'd like them to be. Your goal is to get positive reviews on your book. The last thing you want to deal with is some reviewer that is far too busy and overwhelmed, or worse yet, doesn't take you seriously.

Understanding that reviewers are busy people with real lives and families outside of all their review tasks, it's important to notice how often they review books. It is also advised to read the details of what they expect when you submit your review to them. This should not be an antagonistic relationship between the judge of a book and its author. It should be a mutually acceptable, professional agreement between someone who will read your book with an objective eye and state publically and clearly their unbiased opinion about it, and an author seeking an honest and professional review for his manuscript.

One way to find reviewers for your book is to create a list of them, and then send your book out to as many reviewers as possible, tailoring your requests to their individual requirements, while hoping for the best. It's not optimal, because you never know what you're going to get when you do that, and it might be an unwarranted negative review, because some reviewers aren't exactly all that nice, and for whatever reason, they make it a little more difficult for the writer submitting reviews. At times this can feel like sending out a form letter, but if you're a writer, and obviously you are, because you are submitting your book for a review, your request for a review needs to be an actual sample of your writing, not merely a request and prayer for a review from some randomly selected reviewer.

Many reviewers will sign up on some type of reviewers list, so they are easy enough to find if you take the time to go through their catalog. I'm on the Indie View List, and have received several review requests from authors who have found me there. Twitter is also a good place to search for and find book reviewers, as well as resources to help you find the perfect reviewer for your book. Google has several dedicated communities for book reviewers and book lovers on Google+. The Book Blogger List is also a good site to find lots of reviewers for your book.

Dealing with reviewers shouldn't be intimidating or frustrating at all, providing you remember that there are real people behind all those reviews. Since most submissions are likely to be done via email, requesting reviews from qualified reviewers can be rather time consuming, especially if you are drafting personalized submission requests to each reviewer. Once you send out your request, there's the dreaded waiting period, to see if any reviewers are interested in reviewing your book.

It's not really a pet peeve of mine, but the majority of the requests I receive are the same. Creativity is extremely limited, as the authors usually submit a copy of the cover, a brief synopsis of the storyline, sometimes a limited bio of the author and some generic terms and expressions, asking me if I have time to review their book. There's nothing personal about most of the requests I receive, which makes me surmise that many authors are sending dozens of requests, without thinking of me as anything more than a possible positive review and perk for the promotion of their book. Balance this out with some of the truly great and inspiring authors I've had the pleasure of working with, and it's easy to understand why some reviewers don't even respond to all the review request submissions they receive.

Paying for reviews is an option available to any writer, though I strongly recommend against this practice. Reviewers who receive payment for their work have no vested interest in actually reading your book, because they didn't exactly choose to read it, and their true motive for doing so is to earn the paycheck that helps pay their bills, provides them with some extra spending money or contributes to their vacation fund. Regardless of why they are getting paid for writing reviews, it's their job, not necessarily their passion and willingness, to help authors promote their books to the top of their genre. You would be much better off investing your time and efforts in a superior marketing campaign for your book, as opposed to paying someone to read and review it, in my opinion and experience as an author and professional reviewer.

Chapter 6: Working with Your Reviewers

Working with and getting to know reviewers should be any author's goal, in my opinion. Both parties work together to promote writers and their books. In order to remain objective and publish an unbiased review, reviewers have the distinct task of remaining professional in their role, whereas authors are commissioned to leave their egos at the door, respecting and appreciating their individual reviewers. I get that you spent hours, days, weeks and months writing and publishing your book. Do you get that I'm going to spend hours and possibly days reading and reviewing it?

Having a positive and healthy relationship with your reviewers can only help you as an author. Each reviewer has the potential to bring new buyers and readers to your front door. Reviewers who post independently on specific review sites, or their own personal blogs, often have their own audience, people who are tuned in and appreciative of the articles they publish in their own rite, so if they publish a review of your book there, they are literally introducing you to their own personal fan base, thereby helping you to expand yours in turn.

Developing a working relationship with your reviewers may be time consuming, but it will only help you in the long run. Even if a reviewer doesn't like your book, if he is willing to respect you as an author, it's still worth it. Reciprocating this respect is vitally important to have an effective and properly functioning relationship, where the reviewer appreciates the opportunity to review your book, because you're a considerate author, and you appreciate the opportunity to work with such a fine reviewer.

Investing in your relationship is certainly not a bad thing. Chances are you'll never be overly chummy with your reviewers, because both of you are way too busy to foster much more than a "Thank you for your book submission," and "Thank you for considering my book for review." All things considered, however, you might procreate a mutually beneficial working relationship, if you take the time to nurture it. This is an important element in selecting your reviewers, because as every writer knows, the market is completely saturated these days. There are so many books out there; getting reviews is tough. If you can somehow cultivate a decent relationship with a couple of well established and friendly reviewers, you simply can't lose, because even if they don't particularly like one of your books, at least they will be kind about the reasons why.

It's not always easy to do, and some reviewers don't want to actually work with authors. They simply want to read and pass judgment on book submissions, opting to stay impartial by not getting to know the authors of the books they choose to read. I thought that way once, until I realized it was my own ego getting in the way of a mutual goal to see excellent books rise to the top of the charts. Impartiality doesn't depend on anonymity, and it's much easier to review books when I have a sense of who wrote them and why. Multiple factors go into the production of a book. Authors don't write blindly in a cave. They incorporate all sorts of resources and draw on all sorts of emotions when they are writing. Reviewers do the same thing when they are reading and writing their reviews. How the book makes them feel is an essential element that will help or hinder the reviewing process, which is why I contend that authors and reviewers need to work together, for the mutual benefit of all parties concerned, namely the author, the reviewer and the prospective audience.

Chapter 7: Preparing Your Review Request

As mentioned in Chapter 5, the majority of the review requests I receive are rather similar. It is my contention, however, that if an author can't write a simple essay full of heart and soul about the book they published, then maybe they shouldn't be seeking reviews from people who are going to actively spend so much time with their manuscripts. I get that there are hired firms who actively seek reviewers of books for the authors who hire them, and I understand that form letters containing limited and standard information helps streamline their process, so that doesn't bother me at all, because if authors are willing to pay a firm to help them qualify their reviewers, at least they are doing something positive to find the best reviewer for their book.

When you prepare your review request for a possible reviewer, take the time to think about why you wrote the book, who you hoped would read it, why this book is important and how this book will have an impact on those who experience it. Once you've done this, start writing your essay. You know the finer details of your book, and you know who, what, when, where, why and how in this book. Take the time to share the story behind the story, delving into the characters and overview not as a synopsis, but as friends in a place you've grown extremely fond of while you worked on this manuscript.

Preparing your review request should be an intimate exercise, where prospective reviewers get a feel for the heart, soul, guts and glory that went into the making of your book. It's one of the things I find so rewarding in my venture of writing book promotions on my blog. Authors are asked to send me as much information as they can, and share some of the intimate details behind the development and publication of their book. If only they would do something similar when they submit their reviews, because these are the stories of their inspirations, the tales of the people who influenced their work and the affinity of their character and moral compass.

This is the insight I need, to get excited about reading and writing a possible book review. Anyone can submit the basics and provide a generic description and book review request. Anyone can send a book to a potential reviewer. Only one person, however, can delve into the heart and soul of any author's work, the very same person who takes pride in the accomplishment of publishing that book, the person who will defend the honor of that book and feel a little slighted when everyone else doesn't quite understand the full meaning or potential of that book. That person is you, the author of that book, which is why you are the only one uniquely qualified to write a review submission request that energizes and excites a prospective reviewer.

You have to get outside of yourself on this one. You have to extend the boundaries of writing and publishing your book, into the marketing and promotion of your book. You can't do this by being ordinary and plain. Your book is not ordinary and plain. It is one of a kind, unique and special. As the author, you are distinctly adept at selling this masterpiece you created. Publishing your book is the first step. Getting people to read your book takes time, patience and effort. Selling people on why your book should be read by the masses cannot be an ordinary, office work task, where you find possible reviewers and submit generic, boring review requests in the hopes that someone, anyone will decide to read your book and publish a review for you.

Part 3: Book Review Business

Chapter 8: Publishers and PR Firms

Securing book reviews is big business for literary publishers and PR Firms. They need book reviewers to help promote their books and clients. As an established book reviewer, I receive dozens of emails regularly, asking me if I'd like to be added to their list of reviewers willing to write reviews for their authors. I'm on a few lists and receive notifications of books that need to be reviewed by them quite regularly, though neither of us have a contingent, business relationship. I'm not an employee or consultant of theirs, and have positively no relationship with them, other than the fact that they send me opportunities to receive books to review, in their efforts to secure professional reviews for their authors. I do not get paid for any service or book review I write, based on books they suggest that I ask be sent to me.

It truly amazes me when publishers and PR firms make it difficult for me to work with authors, or receive the books I ask to review. It's to their benefit if I review their books, so they should make this as easy as possible for me. Supply and demand is the opportune phrase here, because there are way more books out there, than there are reviewers to read them and write quality, professional reviews.

This is why I personally believe authors need to secure some of their own book reviews. When it comes to each particular book they publish, they're not in the business of building their own business. They are in the business of sharing their manuscript with others, in the hopes of having as many people as possible read it. Authors are the one's who can best sell and market their books to the public, because they have the inside scoop and passion necessary to do so.

I get that book publishers need to add customers to their database, but reviewers are not customers.

Publishers need to separate and compartmentalize their tasks, understanding that book reviewers aren't in the business of purchasing the books they are selling. We are book reviewers performing a service, oftentimes free of charge, to authors. We are not in the business of promoting book publishers, bookstores and PR firms. Ours is a service to authors, which is why it helps to have a personal relationship with the person who wrote the book.

It also helps to make the book readily available to reviewers, without expecting reviewers to do a bunch of legwork, jumping through hoops, clicking on links and providing personal information in an effort to receive a book. If you're book is that good, that you can get quality reviewers to go to that much trouble, more power to you, but as a reviewer with limited time to read and review all the books I receive, I find it difficult to believe you will get many takers from professional reviewers this way.

If you are an author who has a publisher or has hired a PR firm to help with the marketing and promotion of your book, it is in your best interest to understand the intricate details of how they operate. Your name is on the book. If their name is on the publicity, or if they're the ones seeking reviews for you, it can't hurt to know exactly how you and your book are being represented to those who are being exposed to your book for the first time.

I've actually contacted a PR firm or two and let them know how difficult it was to receive a book, because I believe the author is getting a little short-changed in the experience. To my great dismay,

I've heard back from a publisher or two and been told that I need to adhere to their policies, if I want to receive and review their books. They seem to think that I'm getting something for nothing (a free book), when in actuality, I'm providing a service to them, to help them get more book sales, and I'm not getting paid to do it. This is the tail wagging the dog syndrome in my book, and authors need to understand that publishers and PR firms work for them, and since they are getting a cut of the profits, they need to represent their clients in a professional and upright manner, because book reviewers (professional or otherwise) are an important element in the success or failure of any book. You definitely don't want to bite the hand that could help promote your book to the next level, even if they didn't find your book to be the best one they've ever read.

Chapter 9: Record Keeping

The real work of getting book reviews isn't finding possible reviewers, writing query letters or even submitting your requests to have your book reviewed. As with any good business, keeping accurate records is vitally important to your success as an author, so you know and can follow up with potential book reviewers, or submit to new possible book reviewers, should the need arise.

The first set of records you need to keep is the details and stats of your book. This is important because in many cases, you will need to provide it to those interested in reviewing your book. Things you should include in this set of records is background information, synopsis of book, page and word count, date of publication, ISBN number, publisher and/or publishing platform, available book formats, price, previous review links, availability and date available for pre-sale or sale, photos of book cover and author, plus some brief biographical information about the author. All of these things need to be readily available upon request for your book reviewers, along with various formats of your actual book you can send, should the reviewer decide to read your book.

Other sets of records you might find helpful are spreadsheets of reviewers and their submission requirements, information on your submissions, responses and lack of responses from reviewers you've submitted your request to, dated follow-up information on your review submissions, and appreciation (thank you notes) to those who graciously took the time to read and review your book.

Along with all of this, it is advised that you link to your book reviews on your own site and blog, sharing the work of the reviewer with your audience and fan base. You can also help promote their review via your own social networks, because both of you deserve kudos for the work you do, and reviewers want their reviews read and shared as much as you want your book bought and read. A little appreciation goes a long way. Reviewing is often a thankless job, where the writer enjoys the boost if it's a good review, and the reviewer moves onto the next book. It really does pay to appreciate those working so hard for you, because in all honesty, they have more than a few books to read, and they chose yours out of all the requests they receive.

Acknowledgements

This book could not have been written without the help of so many wonderful writers I've had the pleasure of working with over the years. They generously answered my questions about what it's like working with reviewers, allowing me to understand how frustrating it can be to deal with some of us, myself included. So many authors came back with necessary insights, both positive and negative, about getting reviews and working with reviewers, and I appreciate each and every one of you.

Writers are a unique group of individuals, one I'm proud to be part of and claim as my own. I learn so much from all of you every day, and I'm truly blessed to get to know so many of you through your books, blogs, social media, email and in person. It is with great appreciation that I thank those writers I didn't reach out to when researching this book, because I'm sure knowing you influenced some of the writing just the same. We touch each other's lives all the time, so often that we fail to recognize where inspiration comes from in the moment.

As a writer, my family wins the patience award when I'm engrossed in reading and writing book reviews, working with authors and writing my own books. It's not my day job, but sometimes that pays the price a bit, especially when inspiration strikes and I simply have to sit down at my computer without a moment to lose. It helps to have the best family in the world, you know the one that supports and encourages me every step along the way.

I'm a writer and I review books. I respect and appreciate authors, with a full understanding of the process of authorship and book production. If you'd like me to consider your book for review, or if you'd like me to consider publishing a free book promotion for you, please send me an email: mjjoachimswriting@gmail.com

If you'd like to know more about the book reviews I publish on my blog, please visit M. J. Joachim's Writing Tips, Reviews and More.

We're all in this together, so we might as well help each other along the way. Thank you for taking the time to read this book. I hope it helps you on your journey. Please feel free to write a review for it, so others might benefit from your experience, and determine if they might like to read it too. Thank you.

www.ingramcontent.com/pod-product-compliance
Lightning Source LLC
Chambersburg PA
CBHW072022290526
45787CB00013B/1756